The Customer Service Toolkit

For a complete list of Management Books 2000 titles
visit our web-site on http://www.mb2000.com

Other books in this series include:

The Communication Toolkit
The Developing People Toolkit
The Human Resources Toolkit
The Learning Toolkit
The Motivation Toolkit
The Systems Thinking Toolkit
The Team Management Toolkit

The Customer Service Toolkit

Practical ways to improve personal and work performance

Stuart Emmett

2000

This book is dedicated to my family – to my wife, the lovely Christine, to our two cute children, Jill and James, and James's wife, Mairead (also cute), and to our totally gorgeous three granddaughters, twins Megan and Molly and their younger sister, Niamh.

First published in 2008 by Management Books 2000 Ltd
Forge House, Limes Road
Kemble, Cirencester
Gloucestershire, GL7 6AD, UK
Tel: 0044 (0) 1285 771441
Fax: 0044 (0) 1285 771055
Email: info@mb2000.com
Web: www.mb2000.com

British Library Cataloguing in Publication Data is available

ISBN 9781852525682

Contents

About this book

In writing this book, I have made best-efforts endeavours not to include anything that, if used, would be injurious or cause financial loss to the user. The user is, however, strongly recommended, before applying or using any of the contents, to check and verify their own company policy/requirements. No liability will be accepted for the use of any of the contents.

It can also happen in a lifetime of learning and meeting people, that the original source of an idea or information has been forgotten. If I have actually omitted in this book to give anyone credit they are due, I do apologise and hope they will make contact so I can correct the omission in future editions.

About the author

My own journey to "today", whilst an individual one, did not happen, thankfully, without other peoples involvement. I smile when I remember so many helpful people. So to anyone who has ever had contact with me, then please be assured you will have contributed to my own learning, growing and developing.

After spending over 30 years in commercial private sector service industries, I entered the logistics and supply chain people development business. After nine years as a Director of Training, I then choose to become a freelance independent mentor/coach, trainer and consultant. This built on my past operational and strategic experience - gained in the UK and Nigeria - and my particular interest in the "people issues" of management processes.

Trading under the name of Learn and Change Limited, I currently enjoy working all over the UK and also on four other continents, principally in Africa and the Middle East, but also in the Far East and South America. In addition to my training activities, I am also involved in one-to-one coaching/mentoring, consulting, writing, assessing and examining for professional institutes' and university qualifications.

I can be contacted at stuart@learnandchange.com or by visiting www.learnandchange.com. I welcome any comments.

Preface

Welcome to this new series of business toolkits designed to improve personal and work performance.

A recent report entitled "The Missing Millions – how companies mismanage their most valuable resource" (source: www.Proudfootconsulting.com) stated that "Poor management in the UK is directly responsible for 60 lost working days per employee per year. And a further 25 days lost annually can also be indirectly attributed to management failing."

That is a total of 85 wasted days per employee every year due to poor and failing management. This is around 30% of a normal working year of 240 available days!

According to the report, the main contributing factors were as follows:

- Insufficient planning and control
- Inadequate supervision
- Poor morale
- Inappropriate people development
- IT related problems
- Ineffective communication

This series of concise guides will provide practical advice in each of these key management areas, to enable managers to get the most out of their teams, and make sure that they stay ahead of the game.

The simple truth is that in order to avoid the incredible 85 wasted days per employee per year referred to above, things must be done better *by management*.

Problems with management will almost always turn out to be people problems. Improving performance is therefore essentially about improving individual and team performance so that, in turn, the organisation's performance is improved.

This will require that, for example, the following are considered:

- Developing a strong strategic vision that is underpinned with learning
- Motivating and developing and releasing the potential of people, as individuals and in teams
- Communicating to people what is expected, what they are rewarded for, how they should deliver results and what results the organisation is looking for.

The earlier mentioned Proudfoot research highlighted several areas that managers can work on to improve performance. These are shown again below with a link to the appropriate Toolkit:

- Insufficient planning and control – see the Systems Thinking Toolkit
- Inadequate supervision – see the Team Management Toolkit
- Poor morale – see the Motivation Toolkit
- Inappropriate people development – see the Developing People Toolkit
- IT related problems – see the Systems Thinking Toolkit
- Ineffective communication – see the Communication Toolkit

It should be appreciated that many of these aspects do inter-relate, and that a single quick fix in one area may not always work very well. The Systems Thinking Toolkit does examine more fully all of the interconnected links of inputs, processes and outputs to be considered when improving performance. Also, the Learning Toolkit is paramount, as improvements can only be made after making changes and change, in turn, is directly associated to new learning.

As we have seen, many of the Proudfoot research aspects are directly people-related. In addition to the specific toolkits mentioned above, the Human Resources Toolkit provides a complete framework for effective human resources management.

Finally, as we all know, no business can survive without customers, and the essential skills of customer service are absolutely vital to the retention and growth of the customer base. The Customer Service Toolkit provides quick and easy advice which will produce startling returns.

Part 1. Customers and Organisations

Customers are what really drive an organisation; unfortunately some organisations seem incapable of recognising that their own performance must match the needs of their customers. Improving service is not actually a choice as survival of an organisation may well depend on it.

In capitalist market economies it is said that the market rules. The market is, however, made up from individual customers buying products and services; it is these individual micro-choices that ultimately determine the macroeconomic patterns. "Let the market decide," the economists say; businesses must sink or swim according to their success in the marketplace. For businesses to survive in a market economy, it is therefore absolutely essential to give customers what they need...

Principles of customer service

Some of the most important principles of customer service are as follows:

- Customers have needs and expectations. The magic comes from going beyond the normal customer expectations and going the extra mile to impress the customer.
- Customer service is a source of competitive advantage. But customers may already be using a competitor's products/service; then the question is, why?
- Customer service is always delivered by people; how they do this is often more important than the product/service actually being delivered.

- Customer service has different levels of service, so how do we experiment with different levels so we can better determine the organisations future?
- Organisations must maximise the customer service experience, so that customers will not only return, but will also encourage others to buy from the organisation (repeat business is a cheaper option than having to get new business).

Using customer service this way may require a new style of management – a style that combines hard quantifiable aspects like target setting and measurement with soft qualitative aspects like communicating and motivating.

Definitions of customer service

Customer service is variously seen as an activity, as a performance measurement and as a philosophy. There is no single definition of customer service. The following five views represent some of the different definitions:

1. Customer service is seen as satisfying needs

- "Customer service is a function of how well an organisation meets the needs of its customers."
- "Customer service is the ability of an organization to constantly and consistently exceed the customer's needs and expectations."

2. Customer service is seen as taking care

- "Customer service is a phrase that is used to describe the process of taking care of our customers in a positive manner."

3. Customer service is seen as keeping promises

- "Customer service is the ability to provide a service or product in the way that it has been promised."

4. Customer service is seen as adding value for customers

- "Customer service is a process for providing competitive advantage and adding benefits in order to maximize the total value to the customer."
- "Customer service is the commitment to providing value-added services to external and internal customers, including attitude, knowledge, technical support and quality of service in a timely manner."

5. Customer service is seen as all aspects of customer contact

- "Customer service is any contact between a customer and the company which causes a negative or positive perception by the customer."

Customer service history

There have been quantum changes in attitudes towards customer service in recent years. It is not so long ago that many firms regarded customers as a necessary evil, sometimes a positive "nuisance". This was in the times when organisations were production-led – when they felt they could take it for granted that customers would buy their products (all they had to do was produce them). This had been the prevailing attitude for many years, and was perhaps best epitomised by the early 20th-century car manufacturer Henry Ford who famously announced that customers could have any colour of car they wanted, as long as it was black.

Here we had organisations being able to easily sell what they produce; the focus was on meeting the needs of sellers needs, rather than the needs of customers.

However, towards the end of the last century this all changed. We now live in a market-led economy where consumers are free to choose between a wide variety of competing products and services. To survive, organisations must now determine what the customers' needs are and what they want to buy. Competition is now found in the majority of sectors, where high product variety and multiple choices are being offered to customers. Supplying organisations now have to try and win market share; it is now customer satisfaction and loyalty that "rule".

Customers' needs now have to be understood and anticipated so that only those products which can be sold are actually produced.

Public and private sectors

Changes in attitudes towards customer service have been seen in both the public and the private sectors. However the dynamics of these two sectors are very different, and the public sector remains predominantly production-led as demonstrated by the following table:

Feature	Public sector	Private sector
Main drivers	Maintain the current service levels due to resource constraints. Political imperatives. "Survival" decisions are up to politicians; the managers "advise". Image and politics. Balance the books.	Growth. Commercial imperatives and customer satisfaction. "Survival" decisions are made by managers. Brands. Make a profit.
Structure	Centralised and bureaucratic – "by the book".	Any type of structure can be found.
Culture	Job for life (security). Little incentive to change. No performance linked pay.	Job insecurity. Continual change. Performance incentives often found.
Ultimate responsibility	Politicians and elected bodies. Cannot go out of business.	Shareholders or "self." Frequent close downs.
Buying	Tendering and long decision making.	Quicker decision making and price

	Price sensitive. Fixed goalposts.	discussions. Less price sensitivity and more emphasis on "value." Goalposts change during negotiations
Marketing issues	Customer already exists and is disgruntled. Users have little choice or no choice about using the service.	Customers have to be "sold". Competition exists and the aim is to get repeat business and retain the customer who can easily go else where.

Source: www.ukhrd.co.uk and the Independent on Sunday

These distinctions are particularly relevant for those parts of the former UK public sector which have been privatised over recent years. These businesses have had to deal with a major shift of emphasis from supply-led management to market-led management where the provision of customer service suddenly becomes paramount.

Now, with the idea that the customer has a choice, these organisations clearly need to be more responsive to customers' needs. In turn, they must look to become more productive and efficient.

While many privatised utilities enjoyed a near monopoly situation in the early years of privatisation, even while the monopolies lasted, competitive pressures mounted.

Monopolies and Competition

In a monopoly situation, the following may be the prevailing view:

- Customers already exist
- Customers are often disgruntled
- Customers are called users
- Customers have no alternative provider/supplier

However, alternatives are always being searched for by customers and consequently it is dangerous even for these organisations to ignore the power of the customer. Additionally, in the UK, many former monopoly suppliers of utility services have been deliberately made subject to competitive pressures. Here, new and variable service level offerings create choice in the marketplace that is driven by competition. With competition therefore:

- Customers have to be found and be "sold" to
- Customers can choose from competing suppliers
- Organisations aim is to get repeat business and retain the customer as the customer can easily go else where
- The customer "rules"

Quality and customer service

An organisation that delivers consistent good customer service is usually seen as being a quality company. Indeed, quality has many parallels with customer service, as quality management represents the involvement and commitment of everyone, in continuously improving work processes, to satisfy the requirements and expectations of all internal and external customers.

Quality is therefore that "something" which

- meets customer requirements
- is fit for purpose
- delights the customer
- is of value to the customer

The role of the customer is again seen in the following ten basic principles of Quality Management:

1. Agree customer requirements
2. Understand and improve customer/supplier chains
3. Do the right things
4. Do things right first time
5. Measure for success
6. Pursue continuous improvement
7. Ensure that management lead
8. Provide proper training
9. Communicate more effectively
10. Recognise successful involvement

Total Quality Management (TQM) is an approach towards larger-scale company change and improves existing processes and functions. TQM needs strong direction and must be led from the top. It also needs commitment and involvement from all. TQM is therefore about:

- Customers setting the standards
- Reducing total cost
- Continuous improvement
- Strategic change, led by managers
- Doing all of the right things that add value
- Involving everyone
- Avoiding waste and eliminating errors

TQM is not about:

- Meeting only our own standards
- Compromising quality
- Control
- Quality experts being the only ones who check what is done
- Luxury

Part 2. The Importance of Customer Service

We have already established that customer service is fundamentally about satisfying customer needs. Getting this right will enable an organisation to view whether it has a competitive advantage with its customers (who may be either external or internal).

Whether serving external or internal customers, customer service needs to be a total offering. Products and services have different aspects and the relative importance of each will be discussed in this section.

Customer needs

The ability to provide a solution to customers' needs is more important than any other features of the product or service. So what are these needs? For example, why do we buy food? Is it for the packaging, the brand, the touch, the feel, the status? All of these may be involved, but fundamentally we buy food to eat, so that we can survive. Survival is the ultimate need for buying food.

Any organisation must know what its customers' expectations are, particularly with regard to

- Attributes of products
- Expectations from services
- Price sensitivity

Then, after considering how these expectations may change over time, an organisation will need to answer the critical question: how do we actually meet the customers' expectations?

Competitive advantage

In the customer-focused market place, organisations need a competitive advantage. They must be better than the competition. In simple terms they can do this either by "doing it better" or by "doing it cheaper".

Consider the following table on cost leadership (doing it cheaper") and service differentiation ("doing it better).

Cost Leadership	Service Differentiation
Standard products produced cheaply	Customer designed products
Production push	Market pull
Flow and mass volume production, with high mechanisation	Job shop production with low mechanisation
Low inventory	Flexible and varied inventory
Focus on productivity	Focus on creativity
Stable planning	Flexible planning
Centralisation	Decentralisation
Standardisation	Bespoke and one-off's

As "supply chains now compete, not individual companies" (after: Professor Martin Christopher), then organisations will need to:

- Segment customers – we will look at this soon.
- Have good relationships with customers and suppliers and connect "cognitively" – for example, to have visibility of demand, or to release "hidden" supplier innovation. Again we return to this later.
- Use technology that can "enable" and "connect the data".
- Recognise there is global competition, meaning a growth of alliances.

Internal customers

Customers cn be either external or internal. Whilst many have no problem with understanding about external customers (the customer who make pay days possible), many have a poor understanding when it comes to dealing with internal customers. An internal customer may be any of the following:

- Board of directors e.g. as sponsors of a project
- Manager(s)
- Employees
- Users e.g. other departments who may be local or global

Additionally, they may be a supplier in one transaction but a customer in another transaction.

There are numerous types of internal supplier/customer relationships – for example in the office, the passing on of paperwork to the next person; in manufacturing, the passing of a sub assembly to another for completion into a finished product.

If each supplier would view the next connection in line as a customer and treat them accordingly, then relationships would change for the better, and overall the ultimate end service to the final customer would be "perfect."

Total customer service

Top leadership must have the commitment to serving customers, and customer-focused procedures will need to be in place. We will look at the setting of service standards and marketing shortly, all of which will need active management support and using individuals that have the knowledge and skills and desire, to be totally customer focused. In this regard, the following checklist will help.

Customer focus checklist

- Are customer requirements communicated to service employees?

- How are changing requirements of customers captured?

- Do people have an appropriate timeframe to respond to customer needs?

- Do people anticipate customer expectations?

- Is customer retention a priority?

- Do we encourage the satisfaction of internal customers?

- Do we pay particular attention to personal service?

- Are customers encouraged to complain?

- Are customer complaints measured?

- Is delivery performance measured?

- Is the customer satisfaction level measured?

- Are major/loyal customers rewarded?

- Is the quality of relationship with customers measured?

Based on Source: Adebanjo and Kehoe (2001) An evaluation of factors influencing teamwork and customer focus Managing Service Quality Vol. 11 No. 1 pp49-56

What is important to accept in providing total customer service, is that the customer is:

- the business
- the most important person we have contact with
- what we depend on
- who pays our wages
- the purpose of what we do
- part of our business
- a human being with feelings and emotions
- not one to win arguments with
- someone who can build our business and give us a competitive advantage

Therefore:

- We must know who they are
- We must know what they need
- We must anticipate their changing needs
- We must develop a long term relationship

All customers are driven by needs and when a need is not met, then this becomes a problem that causes a customer to look for solutions.

Therefore any feature of a product or service that solves their problem will be perceived as a benefit. In turn, any feature that does not solve the customer's problem will be seen as a waste.

From the customer's perspective, any money, time and effort spent in finding a solution to satisfy their need is seen as a cost. Customers look for solutions that give them value. They will buy, if they believe the benefits (or the value), exceeds the cost of the product or service.

Finally, individual managers in organisations can appreciate that if customer service works well, then for them personally, this will mean:

- Job satisfaction
- Job achievement
- More friendly contacts
- Reduced complaints
- Less fire fighting

Products and services

There are some important differences to consider here.

Products

Products are those things that satisfy a want or need and have:

- **Features** – characteristics beyond the product's basic functioning
- **Performance** – the output levels of its operation
- **Conformance** – how far the product's design and operating characteristics match the requirements
- **Durability** – the product's expected operating life
- **Reliability** – the probability that a product will not malfunction or fail within a specified period of time
- **Reparability** – the ease of fixing a product that malfunctions or fails
- **Style** – how well the product looks and feels to the buyer

Products have a lifecycle, as shown by the following diagram:

Error! Objects cannot be created from editing field codes. The following stages show the connections of customer service to both the product lifecycle and to the organisations functions:

Launch/introduction

- Product design and development is critical involving customer need assessment
- Many design changes
- Short production runs with high production costs
- High stock levels
- High levels of product promotion

Emerging/growth

- Forecasting demand is critical
- Reliability of product and processes
- Competitive improvements and options
- Capacity issues
- Distribution and availability is important

Established /maturity

- Standardisation
- Minor product changes
- Optimum capacity and stock levels
- Stable processes
- Longer production runs
- Product improvements and cost cutting

Decline

- Little product differentiation

- Cost cutting
- Overcapacity in the industry
- Line item pruning
- Reduce capacity

Withdrawal

- The end of the cycle

Services

Services are the performance of an action by one person for another that does not result in ownership. Services are an intangible exchange that may or may not be connected to a physical product; they are perishable and cannot be stored. The performance is often highly variable and unreliable. Services are therefore:

- Intangible:
    - they cannot be seen, tested, touched, felt etc
    - they have to be experienced/bought
- Produced and consumed at the same time
- Highly variable
- Perishable and cannot be stored

Services involve the following:

- **Delivering** – how the product or service is delivered to the customer
- **Installing** – the work done to make a product or service operational in its planned location
- **Training** – enabling the customer's employees to use products properly and efficiently

- **Consulting** – providing data, information systems and advisory services that the seller offers
- **Repairing** –the provision of repair service available to buyers of the company's product.

The Boston Matrix

This famous 2x2 matrix provides a view of how market dynamics and market share reflect the lifecycle of products and services.

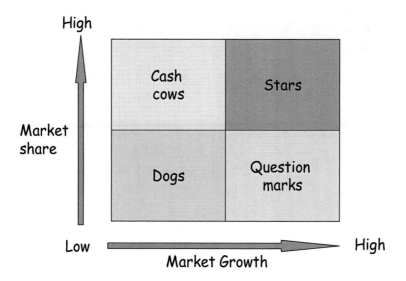

Companies are classified according to the rate of growth of their market, and their own share of that market.

Most products or services start their life as **"question marks"** with a low market share in a healthy growing market. High costs are involved and a decision on payback potential, research, investigation and evaluation will be awaited.

Successful products or services then typically progress to become "**stars**", with a high market share in a still growing market. Because the market is still growing and dynamic, significant ongoing costs are incurred to protect and increase market share.

At the market reaches maturity, successful products or services can ease off on capital spend, and so become "**cash cows**" which can be milked to provide investors with a healthy cash return on their investment – the ultimate goal of all businesses.

The fourth category, "**dogs**", represents the type of doomed product or service which has a low market share in a low growth markets. These products or services are likely to be draining the organisation of cash and using up too much management time. They may be a previous cash cow that is at the end of its product life cycle or, may be a question mark or star that has not made it.

Part 3. Customers and Marketing

> "Marketing is so basic that it cannot be considered a separate function. It is the whole business seen from the point of view of its final result, that is, from the customer's point of view. Business success is not determined by the producer but by the customer."
>
> (Source: Peter Drucker)

Marketing is the process of defining, developing and delivering value to carefully chosen customers, where value is defined by customer needs, perceptions, expectations and use systems. In turn, value is developed around the firm's distinctive competences and is delivered by managing expectations and building long-term relationships.

The marketing mix

The marketing mix describes the mix of issues which affect a product or service's marketing profile. Often described in terms of the six "P's", the mix can be broken down into the following headings:

Product/service

- Features (physical, service, psychological)
- What does it "look like"?
- What will be delivered?
- Description, including benefits
- Value to the customer/ WIIFM (what's in it for me)?
- Customisation/tailoring?

Place

- Distribution channels – how to get products to the marketplace e.g. direct, via wholesalers, via retailers, etc.
- Market positioning and competition in the marketplace
- Inventory levels – where and what format to hold?
- Physical distribution management or logistics – the moving of products to the marketplace
- Internet marketing and "e" shopping

Physical facilities

- Premises
- Impacts and impressions given to visitor/users
- Stationery/PR materials and presentation/appearance

Price
- Cost-plus process, or market-based prices?
- Competition pricing
- Customer perceptions and expectations

Promotion

- Communications (two-way)
- Moving through stages of customers being unaware-aware-comprehension-conviction-action
- Using negotiation/persuasion

People

- Image, such as how they look and "come over"
- Skills and experiences – here the way people are managed must reflect the giving of good service to customers
- Attitudes and behaviour shown towards customers

Working through the "P's" will show the basis of customer's needs and the resultant customer segmentation required.

Customer segmentation

The marketing mix has to be applied in different ways, as not all customers are the same. As we will see later, "perception is reality" – different types of customer have different perceptions of the product, and different needs. To adjust our marketing mix for each customer type we need first to segment the customers into categories.

The following questions can be asked:

- How should we segment, for example:
    - Profitability derived from customer
    - Demand/unit sales/volume derived from customer
    - Payment history/credit rating
    - Customer growth/future potential
    - Customer loyalty
    - Customer needs (this has to be a highly recommended method for segmentation)

- For each segment:
    - Is it viable?
    - How does it differ from other segments?
    - Is it profitable?
    - Who is the decision maker
    - How do they decide?

Such segmentation can use names as follows:

- Standard product/service
- Segmented standard
- Customised standard
- Tailored customised
- Pure customised product/service

Segmentation may also be exploited by offering alternative packages, for example offering different delivery times and discounts for small and large orders. An example might be:

- Small orders are delivered within two days with a high price
- Large orders are price-competitive with agreed lead times that are guaranteed

This type of segmentation can also be applied to service levels, as not every customer will require the same level of service. This principle is accepted and applied, as we find with first or second class postage stamps; first class, business class or economy class air travel, and so on. Selling the right service is important.

In inventory management, the principle is also well established, with varied levels of stockholding of products are held according to relevant customer needs (some customers requiring order fulfilment than others). An example might be:

- "A" customers get 95 % service in terms of availability from the stocking of products
- "B" customers get 90 % service
- "C" customers get 85% service

This varied service level also relates to the cost of providing the service – in this case, the cost of holding the relevant amount of stock (including wastage costs for any resulting surplus or obsolescent stock). The following graph describes the typical relationship between cost and service levels where demand is random (unpredictable).

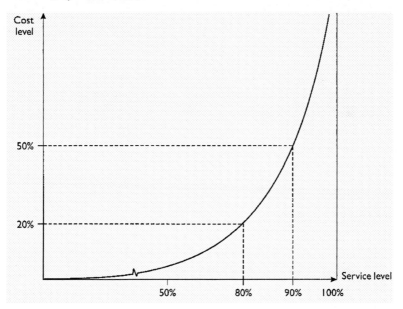

It will be seen that the relationship between cost and service is not linear, but exponential. Higher levels of service require a disproportionately higher level of cost, so that an increase in service level from 90% to 95%, for example, may cost more than twice as much as an increase in service level from 85% to 90%. There is obviously a trade-off between cost and service which must be carefully judged. (However, by changing the underlying systems, there may sometimes be ways to improve service and reduce cost at the same time – see the Systems Thinking Toolkit.)

Organisations need therefore to address the following questions:

- What do we (or can we) offer, in terms of product features and service performance?
- What benefits will our offer have – for example, lower total costs, risk avoidance, increased service, higher quality, marketplace advantage, added value, etc.?
- How does our offer match the customer's requirements and expectations?

In this latter regard, we should always appreciate that customer expectations are often determined or influenced by the other suppliers of the product/service. We may find we are competing with more responsive competition. Customer expectations are therefore continually evolving, changing and growing. This is one the principles of the "market".

Market changes

Market changes are continual, and consequently organisations must also continually examine their markets. To keep abreast of market developments you should routinely ask yourself the following questions:

- Who needs my product/service?
- Why do customers need my product/service?
- What is it about my product/service that is unique for my customers?
- How do my customers differ?
- How do customers differ in how, when, where and why they buy, receive and use my product/service?
- What different forms can my product/service take?

- How can I satisfy whatever customers want from my product/service?
- Where do customers need my product/service?
- How can I provide my product/service wherever customers want it?
- How do customers need my product/service delivered to them?

Organisations need to continually examine their market and customer base and must ensure that they communicate with customers effectively.

Effective customer communication

Communication has been variously defined as:

- "Sharing information between people"
- "Exchanging of ideas that require a reaction"
- "The sending and receiving of verbal and non-verbal messages"
- "The art of being understood"
- "The prevention of misunderstanding"

It takes two to communicate; it is a two-way process. One-way telling, for example, is not communicating. Communication is an active and not a passive process with sharing and exchanging that signifies active involvement between people. As NLP practitioners have noted, "the meaning of communication is in its effect." Communication must always have a result.

Communication ideally should always be clear, direct, short and simple as possible and if important enough, should be done in person by using more than one communication method, with reinforcement and repetition.

For more on communication, please see the Communication Toolkit.

Part 4. Delivering Customer Service

It is important to have good relationships when dealing with customer service. Relationships are always at least two-sided – for example, between a supplier and a customer. How relationships work in practice can obviously vary enormously.

Relationships

A change from more arms-length transactional relationships to more collaborative relationships will reflect a move towards more adaptive relationships. Consider the following questionnaire:

Combative or collaborative customer relationships Score 1 to 10 as follows: 1= totally agree with list A, 5= neither, 10=totally agree with list B			
	List A	**List B**	**Score**
Customers are:	Users	Partners	
Approach with customers:	"Attack/Defend"	Collaborative and problem solving	
Dependency:	Independent	Inter-dependence	
Expected Outcome:	Win/lose, Own survival	Win/win, Mutual survival	

Score: From 4 to 40 = _____

Assess your scores as follows:

4 to 19:   List A favoured: Combative approach
20:         Totally neutral
21-40:   List B favoured: Collaborative approach

This relationship area has been more fully covered in "The Relationship Driven Supply Chain" by Emmett and Crocker (2006), from which the following extract is taken.

An "ideal-typical" comparison follows:

Transactional relationships	Collaboration relationships
Contacts with suppliers	
Short-term	Long-term
Multi-sourcing	Single-sourcing
Distant and Contractual relationships	Close and collaborative relationships
Little commitment beyond the contract	Involvement and "shared destiny"
Information exchanged is orders	Information is shared including forward strategy
Trust is not needed	Trust is essential
Style is competitive, win/loose, power base is combative with command/control behaviour	Style is collaborative, win/win, power base is non existent with honest, open and truthful (HOT) behaviour

Price/Risk	
Price orientation	Total cost of ownership
Price dominates	Shared destiny dominates
One way	Two way exchanges
Customer demands sensitive data	Exchanges of sensitive data
Customer keeps all cost savings	Mutual efforts to reduce costs, times and waste
All risk with supplier, the buyer risks little	Shared risk and benefits
"What is in it for me"	"What is in it for us"
Short term	Long term

Negotiations	
Strong use of ploys in negotiations	Mutual gains "rule" discussions
Power based	Equality based
Win/lose	Win/win
"One off" deals	"For ever" together
Walk in and out of, change is easy	Difficult to break, change is difficult
Easy to set up	Difficult to set up
Adversarial and maybe inefficient for one party	Challenging to implement and continue
"Partnershaft"	Partnership

Inter Personal Relationships	
No personal relationships	Strong personal relationship
Separated/arms length	Close/alliance
Low contact/closed	Shared vision/open
Predatory power based	Proactive and more people based
Hierarchical /superior subordinate	Equality
Blame culture	Problem solving "gain" culture
Alienated employees	Motivated employees
Trust	
Trust is based on what the contract says (contractual trust)	Trust is based on goodwill, commitment and co-operation
Little ongoing trust	Continual trust plus risk/benefits sharing
Power based "spin"	Pragmatic "tough" trust
Controls	
Strong on tactical/ departmental controls	Strong on marketing strategy and supply chain alignment
High formal controls	Self controlled
Rigid contracts	Flexible contracts
Technical performance and the specifications "rule"	Work beyond just "one" technical view
Resource and capacity capabilities	Mutual long term capabilities
Measure by non compliance	Both measure and agree remedial action

The change from transactional methods to collaborative approaches goes beyond the technical issues and fully embraces the soft skills.

The view and belief here from sponsors of collaborative approaches is that if all players work well together, a lot more would get done, more efficiently and more effectively. The evidence for this from basic relationship principles is over-whelming.

The UK Audit Commission (Source: The Audit Commission: A Fruitful Partnership: effective partnership working) has used use the term 'partnership' to describe a joint working arrangement between suppliers and customers where the partners:

- are otherwise independent bodies;
- agree to achieve a common goal;
- create a new organisational structure or process to achieve this goal, separate from their own organisations;
- plan and implement a jointly agreed programme;
- share relevant information;
- pool risks and rewards.

In respect of supplier/customer collaboration, then the following summary is relevant:

Deciding to go into partnership

Ask yourself the following questions

- Does this organisation have clear and sound reasons for being involved in partnerships?

- Are changes in behaviour or in decision-making processes needed to avoid setting up partnerships with only limited chances of success?

If the answer to either question is positive, you should consider going down the partnership route.

Operating efficiently and effectively

To make the most of the partnership ensure that:

- Partners share the same main objectives for the partnership
- Partners know where the boundaries between the activities of the partnership and of their own organisations lie
- Appropriate actions are taken to build and maintain trust between partners

Reviewing success

Routinely asses the ongoing effectiveness of the partnership by answering the following questions:

- Does each partnership have a shared understanding of the outcomes that it expects to achieve, both in the short and longer term?
- What means have been identified for measuring the partnership's progress towards expected outcomes and the health of the partnership itself?
- Has the partnership identified its own performance indicators and set jointly agreed targets for these?

- Are the costs of the partnership known, including indirect and opportunity costs?
- Are these costs actively monitored and weighed against the benefits that the partnership delivers?

Customer touch points

Once we have an order from a customer, then the following process is involved.

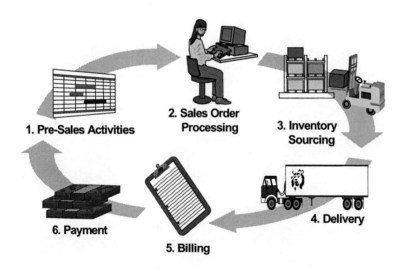

1. Pre-Sales Activities
2. Sales Order Processing
3. Inventory Sourcing
4. Delivery
5. Billing
6. Payment

Note that all of these steps represent touch points with customers.

Customers deal with many different people in an organisation and each customer contact is a touch point. Each touch point provides an opportunity to:

- exceed customer expectations
- provide excellent service to customers
- create the right customer perceptions
- show how efficient you are
- lead to conflicts, angry and unhappy customers

What must never be forgotten is that customers are always buying experiences and that everything done for customers is part of that experience – an opportunity for your staff to differentiate and make a difference.

Making a difference

Two men were walking along the beach. Millions of crabs had been washed ashore from a wild seas storm the night before. One of the men picked up a crab and threw it into the sea. The other man said "that won't make any difference", to which came the reply "it will to that crab".

Lesson: Small things can make a difference to someone

It is always people who deliver customer service; all of the associated touch points must be properly managed.

Determining good customer service

We all have a view of good service. Consider for example, what happened last time you walked into a restaurant:

- How were you greeted?
- How promptly were you attended to?
- How do you think you were regarded by the person serving you?
- How did you feel about this?
- Did the service meet your expectations?
- Has that experience affected your future dealings?

As another example, think of two or three companies you know that have a reputation for good service. What it is that gives these companies their good reputation? Your answers reflect your perception of good service.

Meanwhile, the following questions can be asked;

- As a customer, what would you say about your company?
- How do you encourage customer loyalty?
- How do you handle complaints?
- How often do you respond to the same problems?
- How many customers have you lost in the last three years?
- Why did these happen?
- What are the strengths and weaknesses of your customer service?
- How do you know your customer service is good?

Does the organisation...

- do what has been promised?
- respond quickly?
- have positive employee attitudes?
- proactively communicate?
- include all of the extras?
- look good?

Are we...

- reliable?
- knowledgeable?
- honest and open?
- attentive to detail?
- nice people to deal with?

Answers to these questions will help us to focus on our customer service offering. Ultimately, our offering will need to satisfy what customers expect from us.

Customer satisfiers

All customers will expect as a minimum, the following:

- Reliability
- Responsiveness
- Accessibility
- Accuracy

Providing customers with the above will prevent them from being dissatisfied. However these will not, by themselves, provide the fullest possible satisfaction – to do this, and to avoid any you will also need:

- Courtesy
- Empathy
- Exceptional quality
- Good people relationships
- Delivery of value
- Good complaints handling

Customer perception

One of the obvious difficulties in meeting customer's expectations is that "Perception is Reality". The way that customers perceive you is the only reality that matters to them. Therefore, we are entering into variability and subjectivity. Everything done for customers affects the customer's perception of your organisation – and different customers can perceive the same service levels differently.

It is particularly important to remember that attitudes and feelings will all affect the way any service delivery is going to be perceived. This will require flexibility from management, such as giving discretion to staff to deal with customers and not relying only on standard and fixed structural procedural manuals and guidelines.

Customers are individuals and organisational procedures must support this. Service is all about delivering not only what it is like doing business with your organisation but also with you personally. Feelings and attitudes are important.

The importance of attitudes

Please consider the following diagram

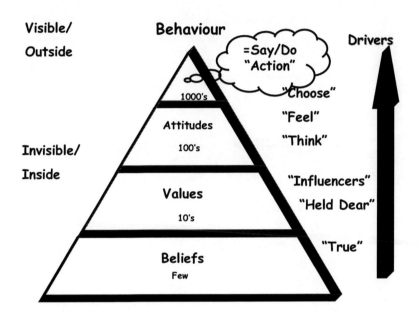

Our attitudes are underpinned by our beliefs and values, all of which will work through into how we behave (defined here as what we say or do).

We will therefore tend to judge from our perspective alone and will not always consider the other parties fully enough.

Good customer-focused people will therefore have a deep belief that customer service is important; they will value and lead by example. This belief will work through into their attitudes and be shown and reflected by what they say and what they do. Good customer-focused people will:

- pull more than push
- be a two-way communicator
- makes concessions ("I think this, but what do you think?")
- problem-solve
- explore interests
- believe in partnership

Customer complaints

Complaints from customers are found when:

- their expectations are not met
- inflexible service has been received
- mistakes have been made
- communications are poor
- delays have been made in delivery
- customers feel they are dealing with unprofessional people

There are, of course, some benefits in receiving complaints, as they give an opportunity to reverse perceptions and to then delight the customer.

When handling complaints, it is therefore important not to:

- be defensive
- pass on the customer to someone else
- leave them waiting for a reply
- make it a drama

If complaints are not handled correctly, then not only can this affect you personally (stress, anger, etc.), but you can lose a customer, which creates bad PR. Plus the customer will, for sure, tell others – we know this will happen, because we do this ourselves when we receive poor service.

However, when complaints are handled well, then everyone wins. The customer knows that they matter and feels satisfied, and the process has highlighted problems that you can overcome and solve.

Dissatisfied customers – some reported facts

- A typical business hears from only 4% of its dissatisfied customers
- A survey on customers who "walked" found:
  - 5% were influenced by friends
  - 9% were lured by competitors
  - 14% were dissatisfied with the product
  - 68% quit because of an attitude of indifference toward them, by the owner, manager or some other employee
- A typical dissatisfied customer will tell 8 to 10 people about their problem
- 70% of complaining customers will do business with you again, if you resolve the complaint in their favour
- If you resolve a compliant on the spot, 95% will do business with you again
- The average business spends 6 times more to attract new customers than it does to keep old ones

Handling verbal complaints

When dealing with these, the guidelines are as follows:

- Listen without prejudice. Done well, this alone can resolve the complaint
- Repeat back
- Apologise
- Acknowledge their feelings
- Explain what you will do
- Thank them

Good listeners are the best communicators; listen sympathetically. If necessary, apologise (this is not an admission of guilt). Tell the customer you are sorry that they have experienced a problem. Take responsibility to solve the problem and say what you will do. Obtain the customers agreement to this action and then do ensure that you follow up.

Problem customers

You will often hear people say about certain customers, "They always complain, they are a problem". Yes, they may regularly complain, but why do they complain? After all it costs them time and effort to do so!

What is usually happening here is that it is the person saying "they always complain" who is the one actually causing the problem. Those who see people as a problem can reflect this destructive attitude when they deal with people; they are unable to separate out the person from the problem.

It is important therefore to see problems as a way forward towards succeeding and a way to find remedial action that prevents further problems.

It may help therefore to see problem customers simply as those who have not had their needs met.

However, does this mean that the customer is always right? Frustrated customers will sometimes "embellish", so it is important to ask for specifics. Sometimes they can be abusive, so here check your company policy and be assertive. Finally, there will be some, despite all efforts, that you cannot help and you are happy to lose. However, if you do everything else right, this should represent a very small minority.

Always remember that a problem is a deviation from something that was expected and that improvement is the better side of the "blame/gain" balance.

Having blame or gain viewpoints

Perception is reality, so how we see things is important. Consider the following lists:

List A	List B
"I am right, I know best"	"I would like to know your opinion"
"Listen to me"	"Let me listen to your view"
Seeing obstacles and Problems	Seeing solutions and opportunities
Finding fault	Giving support
Feeling frustrated when with people	Feels calm when with people
Makes others feel guilty	Makes people learn
Looks for who is wrong	Looks for what is wrong
Mistakes are to be Punished	Mistakes are opportunities to learn

List A is all about blame; List B is more about gain. As perception is reality, then seeing complaints as problems will involve you taking more of a blame view.

Service performance

Service performance should always be traceable back to company goals and objectives – so, for example, if a competitive advantage is the speed of delivery, it is important for the company to measure how quickly things get done.

As service is an output to customers, then the measurements of service should always reflect the needs of the customer; for example, what is "success" for them? To develop the measurements, the following steps can be followed:

1. Identify who is the customer
2. Determine the customer needs/requirements
3. What process output does the customer receive?
4. Determine effective measurements or key performance indicators (see below) that link together 2 and 3
5. Understand the key goals of your organisation
6. How do the KPIs in 4 above relate to the key goals of the organisation and fit into the other process of which they are a part?

The purpose of setting measurable objectives is to give guidance on the existing performance, and to "flag up" any needed improvements.

Key Performance Indicators (KPIs)

These are measurable standards, targets, or outcomes that enable us to determine when a process has been done in accordance with expectations. They also provide a benchmark for a comparison of what actually happened (the actual outcome), against what should have happened (the outcome expected).

KPIs can be grouped into the five Q.C.T.D.S.M categories: quality, costs, time, delivery, safety and morale/motivation; the QCTDSM factors that can be used for measurement are as follows:

Quality

- Are products or services delivered to an agreed specification?
- Do you analyse rejects?
- What is the quality of communication and paperwork like?
- What is the quality of relationships with suppliers/customers?
- % of orders with complaints
- % of customers who give repeat business

Examples of Measures:

- Functionality
- Service
- Defects
- Returns
- Rework
- Complaints
- Re-work
- Warranties
- Complaints

Cost(s)

- Are costs kept within agreed limits?
- Are there cost reduction programmes in place?
- Is cost examined in relation to value and service?
- Do we purchase using total acquisition cost of acquisition and total cost of ownership analysis?

Examples of Measures:

- Stock value
- Activities such as labour
- Over time
- Expenses
- Downtime

Time

- Are time standards available, for example relating to the processing of orders (e.g. if the order is received before 1700 hours, then despatched by 1900 hours)
- Response times to incoming communication (e.g. phone response in two rings, emails response in 24 hours, letters in 48 hours)

Examples of measures:

- Time (minutes, hours, days, weeks, months)
- Shift

Delivery/Speed

- Are goods or services delivered at the right time to right place in the right quantity and in the right condition?
- Are goods delivered on time? (e.g. if the order is received before 1700 hours on day one , then delivered by 1200 hours on day two)
- Are products packaged correctly?
- Are telephone queues kept within agreed limits (e.g. not left queuing for more than 3 minutes)

Examples of Measures:

- On time, in full (O.T.I.F)
- Reliability
- Output
- Accuracy of delivery to location
- Tracking steps whilst in transit
- Emergency response

Safety

- What is the accident record?
- How are the legal requirements effectively carried out?

Examples of Measures:

- Accidents
- Suggestions

Morale/motivation

- Are people there because they want to be there or because they have to be there?
- What is the "temperature" of the people interactions?

Examples of Measures:

- Absences
- Lateness
- Staff Turnover rate
- Suggestions
- Job satisfaction
- Promotions

- Training days
- Skill levels
- Appraisal ratings
- Contacts managers/staff

Watch, however, for the danger of measuring only the prescribed KPIs and then ignoring other things that matter, for example:

- answering a phone at the second ring, but ignoring the customer that is standing in front of you
- replying to an email in 24 hours, saying you will respond the next day, but you do not respond
- despatching on time, but the order is short and not in full (or complete)

Service level agreements (SLAs)

These can be defined as the following:

- "A contract that defines the relationship between a supplier and a customer"

- "A negotiated agreement designed to create a common understanding about service"

SLAs set objective targets that prioritise customers' needs and wants, by defining what is acceptable for both customer and supplier. SLAs will therefore attempt to clarify the following:

- What is expected by the customer?
- What the supplier will supply/deliver?
- How often will it be supplied?

- To what quality standards will it be supplied?
- At what price?
- What are the customer's obligations?
- What is the recourse for both parties if things go wrong?

Typical clauses in SLAs are as follows:

- Service description
- Service levels
- Duration
- Reporting levels
- Level monitoring
- Performance standards
- Review meetings/frequency
- Dispute resolution
- Termination

Is the customer satisfied?

The only way to ever find out the answer to this question is to ask customers how satisfied they are with your service. The following methods are available to do this:

- Face-to-face or by telephone surveys, using open questions to get expansive answers or closed "tell me" questions to get specific answers
- Questionnaire surveys, either by post or electronic/web-based. These typically use Yes/No response or a rating on a 1-5 point scale
- Focus group surveys. These involve selecting a group of people who have awareness of your product/service and seeking their opinions

- "Mystery shopper" – the "invisible" visitor who tests your service in the disguise of an ordinary shopper. They may even make a complaint to test how complaints are handled by your people.
- Free phone help/support line
- Planned (but ostensibly random) visits/calls on customers,

Specimen questions that can be asked to customers, especially in surveys, are as follows:

- How often do we do things right the first time?
- How often do we do things right on time?
- How quickly do we respond to your requests for service?
- How accessible are we when you need to contact us?
- How helpful and polite are we?
- How well do we speak your language?
- How hard do you think we work at keeping you a satisfied client?
- How well do we deliver what we promise?
- How much confidence do you have in our products /services?
- How well do we understand and try to meet your special needs and requests?
- Overall, how would you rate the appearance of our facilities, products and people?
- Overall, how would you rate the quality of our service compared to our competitors?
- How willing would you be to recommend us?
- How willing would you be to buy from us again?

One danger of course, with involving customers in completing questionnaires, is that they have others things to do than answer your questions. Additionally, any responses may be hurried and only give loose indications.

However, customer surveys can give vital information on core customer needs. For example, they might show that reliable, predictable response times are rated higher than price, indicating that immediate response can be premium priced etc.

The Mckinsey Quarterly (2003, no. 4) reported that when customers are segmented into what they need, they tend to fall into three categories:

- "Risk avoiders" – who want to avoid non-supply and are not bothered about anything else
- "Basic needs customers" – who want a standard level of service
- "Hand holders" – who want a high reliable service and will pay for the privilege

The customer service focused organisation

To be a customer service focused organisation, you will need to know:

- Who your customers are
- What they expect and need from you
- How well you are meeting these expectations
- How to provide customer care and follow up
- What benefits customers have obtained from your service
- What needs to be done to make improvements
- What are the barriers to making these improvements
- How you can remove these barriers
- How you will know that what you are delivering is exactly what the customer is expecting from you

The following view of a customer service focused and non customer focused organisations shows what is important:

Customer service focus	Non customer focus
Profit comes from customer satisfaction	Profit comes first, then customer satisfaction
Prevents problems	Detects problems
People "rule"	Numbers "rule"
High training spend	Low training spend
Explicit standards	Vague standards
Complaints seen as a chance to learn	Complaints are a nuisance
Run by people working with other people using systems, if appropriate	Runs by systems and procedures and then people

The customer service focused organisation will therefore have the following five key attributes:

- Reliability – providing dependable, accurate performance consistently, in all of the details
- Ownership – showing front-line ownership, so that those who receive complaints are also able to sort them out (it is not unusual for only 5% of complaints to be resolved at

the first point of contact, thus creating delays with dissatisfied customers)

- Responsiveness – showing clear evidence of "willingness to help" (for example, answer letters within 2 days, answer the phone in 5 seconds, answer emails in 24 hours)
- Attitude – showing courtesy, friendliness, empathy and caring by employees for the customer's "unique" requirements
- Appearance – with clean and tidy facilities, equipment, people, etc.

Case study

The following case study gives practical applications on customer service

---

Service Disney-Style

Disney World enjoys a 40% repeat business ratio, with a high emphasis on making the Disney experience pleasurable, knowing that a high proportion of their guests will return.

The Service theme is: "We create happiness by providing the finest in family entertainment."

The Disney System includes a broad philosophy that addresses the following issues:

- Promotion from within
- Treating visitors as "Guests"
- Treating staff as "Cast Members"
- Treating what the guest see as "On-Stage"
- Treating behind-the-scene activities as "Back-Stage"

The Disney people view quality service as "putting yourself in the mind of the guest", with an overall emphasis on attention to detail, and always exceeding the guests' expectations.

All guests are treated as VIPs (Very Individual People).

Measurable criteria, in the following order:

- **Safety** – this is of paramount importance, and is built into everything that happens in Disney World as a primary consideration.

- **Courtesy** – there is a concentration on providing courteous service to the guests, and a general display of cheerful good manners. These include greetings in a host of languages.

- **Show** – there is a "theme" which imparts an implied message in every activity, from eating lunch to taking rides or visiting the attractions.

- **Efficiency** – is never carried out at the expense of the above criteria. For example, the gates of the Magic Kingdom are closed in peak season, once 50,000 guests are inside. This ensures the safety and enjoyment of all.

- **Setting** – relates to the physical environment, such as cleanliness and other objects within the environment. All systems and procedures that affect the environment take into account the fact that guests are continually taking pictures. Therefore lawns need to be manicured, streets kept clean, etc., since photographs invariably highlight the conditions that the guest has experienced. Each cast member takes responsibility for cleanliness in the space that they occupy. Litter is everybody's problem.

- **Delivery** – the Disney theme is generally to combine "thinking" with "doing". The Disney system goes beyond near creative imagination, to the actual implementation of strategies and tactics which are designed to carry out the concepts initially visualised on the drawing board.

It is interesting to note that the Disney management convey the message to all cast members that they do not have "problem guests"; they merely have "disillusioned guests". To this end, various strategies are in place to respond to disillusioned guests. For example if a disillusioned guest had a bad experience with Captain Cook, Peter Pan would respond to the guest offering solutions.

Benefits of good customer service

As has been seen, the road to improving customer service may not be easy; however the benefits can be huge. The following benefits will all make contributions to the survival, well-being and profitability of any organisation:

- Reliable service is a marketable product with a price difference
- Market changes, and many are always coming to most organisations, can be better handled and managed
- Continuous improvement becomes a part of the culture, with innovative and responsive staff; there is a new enthusiasm and support amongst people
- A positive view of your organisation from shareholders, the community and potential employees, with competitors who "fear" your organisation

- Customers see the organisation as:
    - responsive and listening
    - collaborative and sharing
    - understanding what is critical to their own success
    - "good people to deal with"

Conclusion

In the introduction we highlighted several areas that managers can work on to improve productivity. These are shown again below with a link, (in brackets), to the appropriate Business Toolkit.

- Insufficient planning and control (see the Systems Thinking Toolkit)
- Inadequate supervision (see the Team Management Toolkit)
- Poor morale (see the Motivation Toolkit)
- Inappropriate people development (see the Developing People toolkit)
- IT related problems (included in the Systems Thinking Toolkit)
- Ineffective communication (see the Communication Toolkit)
- Poor Human Resources Management procedures (see the Human Resources Toolkit)
- Poor customer service (dealt with in this Customer Service Toolkit)
- Poor training/learning for specific skills and procedures (see the Learning Toolkit)

Readers are encouraged to take advantage of the complete list of toolkits, which complement each other to provide a comprehensive portfolio of concise pocket guides to improved personal and business performance.

References

Adebanjo and Kehoe, 2001: "An evaluation of factors influencing teamwork and customer focus in Managing Service", Quality Vol. 11 No. 1 pp49-56

Audit Commission 1998: "A Fruitful Partnership: effective partnership working"

Peter Drucker 2004: "The Daily Drucker", Harper Business

Emmett and Crocker 2006: "The Relationship Driven Supply Chain" Gower Press

"Independent on Sunday" dated 11 April 1993

The Mckinsey Quarterly 2003 number 4

www.ukhrd.co.uk in March 2000